The Timeless Path To Wealth

Simple Rules for Building Lasting Financial Freedom

Richard Trillion Mantey

Dedication

To my parents —

Thank you for your sacrifices, your wisdom, and your prayers.

You laid the foundation that made this path possible.

And to everyone who's ever felt behind…

This book is for you.

For the quiet moments, you doubted if financial freedom was even possible for someone like you.

For the years you gave your all and still felt stuck.

For the decision you just made — to stop surviving and start building.

May this be the turning point you've been waiting for.

You're not too late. You're right on time.

Acknowledgments

First and foremost, I thank God, the source of all wisdom, clarity, and abundance. Without divine direction, none of this would be possible.

To my family and close circle: your belief in me, even when I doubted myself, gave me the strength to keep showing up. Thank you for your love, patience, and unwavering support.

To the people I've learned from — mentors, authors, entrepreneurs, and everyday individuals who turned their financial struggles into stories of strength — your journeys shaped this one. This book is rooted in lessons from both success and failure, and I'm grateful for every one of them.

To my editor, your sharp eye, thoughtful suggestions, and commitment to excellence helped shape this book into something clearer, stronger, and more powerful. Thank you for refining the message while preserving its heart.

To my readers: thank you for choosing this book out of thousands. You are the reason I wrote this — to remind you that financial freedom is possible, and that your journey can begin right here, right now.

Let this book be more than words. Let it be a wake-up call, a roadmap, and a reminder that wealth begins with intention.

About the Author – Richard Trillion Mantey

Richard Trillion Mantey is a financial clarity coach, entrepreneur, and lifelong student of wealth-building principles that actually work, not just in theory, but in real life.

After years of navigating debt, uncertainty, and the pressure to "do money right," Richard uncovered a timeless set of simple rules that helped him take control of his finances, shift his mindset, and build a foundation for lasting success. Today, he teaches those same principles to people around the world who are tired of chasing trends and ready to build real wealth with confidence.

Through his books, courses, and voice-driven coaching, Richard inspires readers to break free from confusion and start walking the clear, grounded path toward financial freedom — one powerful decision at a time.

When he's not writing or coaching, you'll find him journaling, exploring big ideas, and helping others live with clarity, courage, and intention.

Preface

Wealth is often misunderstood as a privilege reserved for a fortunate few. In truth, real wealth is built quietly, patiently, through small, deliberate choices made every single day. It is not simply a measure of money, but a reflection of freedom, peace of mind, and the ability to provide for the people and causes that matter most. This book is written for those who may have felt overwhelmed, behind, or uncertain about where to begin their financial journey. You will not find complex theories or intimidating jargon here. Instead, you'll discover timeless principles; clear, actionable steps rooted in discipline, resilience, and simple wisdom that anyone can apply, regardless of income or background.

Through real-life stories and proven strategies, you will learn how to reshape your mindset, manage debt, build savings, invest confidently, and protect what you've worked hard to create. This is not about chasing shortcuts or overnight riches. It's about building something solid and lasting. Your journey to financial freedom does not depend on where you start; it depends on your willingness to start. Let these pages serve as your guide to building a future that reflects your highest goals and greatest potential.

Contents

Chapter 1: The Foundation of Timeless Wealth

Understanding Wealth

Wealth is often perceived as an accumulation of money and assets, but understanding its true essence goes far deeper. Wealth encompasses not only financial stability but also emotional richness and the freedom to pursue our passions. Take, for instance, the story of Maria, a single mother who, despite earning a modest salary, built a wealth of experiences and connections that enriched her life and the lives of her children. Her journey illustrates that wealth is not merely about what you have, but about who you become through your experiences.

The science behind wealth shows that our mindset plays an important role in our financial outcomes. Research indicates that individuals with a growth mindset tend to achieve greater financial success than those who see their abilities as fixed. By cultivating a positive relationship with money and viewing challenges as opportunities for growth, anyone can enhance their financial literacy. Consider the tale of James, who transformed his financial situation by embracing learning rather than fearing failure, demonstrating that knowledge and resilience are invaluable assets on the path to wealth.

Building lasting wealth requires not only a shift in mindset but also practical steps. Setting clear financial goals, creating a budget, and investing wisely are foundational practices that everyone can adopt. For example, Sarah and Tom, a couple from a small town, realised their dream of owning a home by diligently saving and learning about investment opportunities. Their story emphasises that consistent, small actions can lead to significant financial achievements over time.

Moreover, it is essential to recognise the power of community and support in our wealth-building journey. Sharing knowledge and resources can amplify our efforts. The narrative of a local co-operative in a rural area, where members pooled their resources to start a business, illustrates how collaboration can lead to collective wealth. Each member not only benefited financially but also strengthened their bonds, fostering a sense of belonging and shared purpose.

Ultimately, understanding wealth is about more than just numbers in a bank account; it is about creating a life of purpose, connection, and fulfilment. By embracing the principles of growth, taking actionable steps, and nurturing our relationships, we can all embark on our unique journeys to financial security. The stories of Maria, James, Sarah, Tom, and many others serve as reminders that wealth is within everyone's reach, irrespective of their starting point, as long as they are willing to learn and grow.

The Mindset Shift

In our journey towards financial security, the most significant barrier we often face is our mindset. Many individuals possess limiting beliefs about money, viewing it as a scarce resource instead of a tool for abundance. This mindset can stem from childhood experiences, cultural narratives, or personal failures. For instance, consider the story of a young woman who grew up in a household that constantly struggled to make ends meet. She believed that wealth was unattainable, and this belief followed her into adulthood, impacting her financial decisions and opportunities. Recognising and transforming these beliefs is the first step towards achieving lasting wealth.

Shift your perspective from scarcity to abundance. This transformation requires intentional effort and practice. Research in psychology suggests that individuals who adopt an abundance mindset are more likely to seize opportunities and take calculated risks. For example, a successful entrepreneur once shared how shifting her mindset allowed her to see potential where others saw obstacles. She learned to view failures not as endpoints but as stepping stones towards her goals. By embracing this shift, she not only improved her financial situation but also enriched her personal life, demonstrating that mindset can indeed shape our realities.

To cultivate an abundance mindset, start by practising gratitude. Each day, write down three things you are grateful for, focusing on the wealth you already possess—be it in relationships, health, or experiences. This simple exercise helps rewire your brain to recognise the abundance around you. Additionally, surround yourself with positive influences, such as books, podcasts, and mentors who embody the mindset you aspire to adopt. Their stories and insights can inspire and reinforce your own transformation, making the journey towards financial security feel more attainable.

Moreover, take actionable steps towards your financial goals. Set clear, achievable objectives and break them down into smaller tasks. This approach not only makes the process less overwhelming but also allows you to celebrate small victories along the way. Each success, no matter how minor, reinforces your new mindset and builds confidence. A man who started saving a mere five pounds a week eventually amassed a significant emergency fund, demonstrating that even small actions can lead to substantial results over time.

In conclusion, the journey to wealth begins with a fundamental shift in how we perceive money and opportunities. By adopting an abundance mindset, practising gratitude, surrounding ourselves with positive influences, and taking actionable steps towards our goals, we can dismantle the barriers that hold us back. Remember, wealth is not merely a destination but a journey shaped by our thoughts and actions. Embrace this mindset shift, and you will pave the way for a secure financial future that truly reflects your aspirations.

Chapter 2: The Power of Financial Literacy

Key Financial Concepts

Understanding key financial concepts is essential for anyone seeking to build lasting wealth. At the heart of these concepts lies the principle of compound interest, often referred to as the "eighth wonder of the world" by Albert Einstein. This principle illustrates how money can grow exponentially over time when reinvested, rather than simply accumulating interest on the initial amount. Imagine a young person investing a modest sum in their twenties; by the time they reach retirement, that initial investment could blossom into a substantial nest egg, demonstrating the power of patience and perseverance in wealth accumulation.

Another crucial financial concept is budgeting, which serves as the foundation for effective money management. A well-structured budget allows individuals to track their income and expenses, ensuring they live within their means while also setting aside funds for future goals. One inspiring story involves a couple who, after realising they were living paycheck to paycheck, decided to embrace budgeting. By meticulously tracking their spending, they identified unnecessary expenses and redirected those funds towards savings, ultimately achieving their dream of homeownership. This narrative exemplifies how discipline and awareness can lead to financial freedom.

The importance of diversification in investment cannot be overstated. Diversification means spreading investments across various asset classes to mitigate risk. A compelling example is the story of an investor who, during a market downturn, suffered significant losses due to a concentrated portfolio. In contrast, another investor who had diversified across stocks, bonds, and real estate remained relatively unscathed. This principle teaches us that by not putting all our eggs in one basket, we can protect ourselves from unpredictable market fluctuations, ultimately leading to a more stable financial future.

Moreover, understanding the concept of passive income is vital for those wishing to create lasting wealth. Passive income refers to earnings derived from investments or business ventures that require minimal labour to maintain. A real-life example is a writer who, after publishing a book, continues to earn royalties long after the initial effort. This demonstrates how creating assets that generate income over time can provide financial security and freedom, allowing individuals to focus on what they truly love.

Lastly, financial literacy plays a pivotal role in navigating the complex world of personal finance. The more informed individuals are about financial products and strategies, the better equipped they are to make sound decisions. A poignant story illustrates this: a young woman, initially overwhelmed by debt, took the initiative to educate herself through books and online courses. Armed with knowledge, she successfully negotiated lower interest rates and developed a repayment plan that ultimately led her to financial stability. This highlights the transformative power of education in achieving one's financial goals.

The Importance of Education

Education is not merely a tool for acquiring knowledge; it is a pathway to empowerment and wealth creation. Individuals who invest in their education are often better equipped to navigate the complexities of financial decisions. For instance, consider the story of Maria, a single mother who, despite facing numerous challenges, pursued her degree in accounting. Through her educational journey, she transformed her life, ultimately securing a stable job that provided her family with financial security.

Scientific studies have shown that higher levels of education correlate with increased earning potential. Research indicates that individuals with a university degree earn significantly more over their lifetime compared to those without. This statistic is not just a number; it represents countless lives transformed through education. Take the case of James, who, after completing his studies in engineering, was able to innovate and lead projects that not only boosted his income but also contributed to societal advancements.

Education also fosters critical thinking and problem-solving skills, essential for making informed financial choices. A well-rounded education encourages individuals to question, analyse, and make sound decisions. For example, Sarah, a graduate in finance, used her knowledge to create a successful investment strategy that allowed her to retire early. Her story exemplifies how education can be a catalyst for financial independence.

In addition to personal stories, it is crucial to highlight actionable steps for those seeking to enhance their financial literacy through education. Start by identifying areas of interest or skills that align with your career goals. Enrol in courses, attend workshops, or seek mentorship from professionals in your desired field. The journey of education is ongoing, and every step taken can lead to greater financial rewards.

Lastly, the importance of education extends beyond individual gain; it contributes to the overall prosperity of society. A well-educated populace creates a robust economy, fosters innovation, and reduces inequality. Investing in education is, therefore, not just a personal endeavour but a societal necessity. By sharing knowledge and resources, we can build a future where everyone has the opportunity to achieve financial security and success.

Chapter 3: Setting Clear Financial Goals

Defining Your Vision

Defining your vision is the cornerstone of building lasting financial wealth. It is the guiding star that illuminates your path, helping you navigate through the complexities of financial decisions. Consider the story of a young entrepreneur who dreamed of creating a sustainable business. She began with a vision of not just making money, but also making a positive impact on her community. This clarity propelled her through obstacles and setbacks, demonstrating the power of a well-defined vision in achieving financial success.

Science supports the notion that having a clear vision enhances motivation and goal-setting. According to psychological research, individuals who articulate their goals are more likely to achieve them. This is because a defined vision creates a mental blueprint, allowing you to visualise your desired outcomes. For example, a study found that people who wrote down their financial goals were significantly more likely to reach them compared to those who did not. Establishing a personal vision is not merely an exercise in dreaming; it is a practical step towards financial security.

To define your vision, start by reflecting on what wealth truly means to you. Is it about financial independence, the ability to travel, or providing for your family? Write down your thoughts and feelings about your ideal financial future. This exercise is akin to crafting a personal manifesto—one that will serve as your reference point when making financial decisions. When faced with choices, you can ask yourself, "Does this align with my vision?" This simple question can keep you grounded and focused on your long-term goals.

Next, share your vision with others. Engaging friends, family, or mentors can provide valuable insights and support. They can challenge your ideas and help refine your vision, making it more robust. For instance, a retired couple shared their vision of travelling the world, which led to them discovering investment opportunities that funded their adventures. By articulating your vision, you not only hold yourself accountable but also invite collaboration and encouragement from your community.

Finally, revisit and revise your vision regularly. As you grow and your circumstances change, so too should your vision. Life events, such as a new job or the birth of a child, can shift your perspective on wealth and security. Adapting your vision ensures it remains relevant and inspires you to pursue your financial goals passionately. Just like the entrepreneur who started with a small idea and evolved her vision into a thriving enterprise, your journey towards wealth is dynamic and ever-changing, requiring you to define and redefine your goals as you progress.

Short-term vs Long-term Goals

Setting financial goals is crucial for anyone wishing to build a secure future, and understanding the difference between short-term and long-term goals is fundamental to this process. Short-term goals often focus on immediate needs or desires, such as saving for a holiday or paying off a credit card. These goals provide quick wins and can boost motivation, as they are usually attainable within a year. For example, a young professional might aim to save a certain amount for a weekend getaway, experiencing the satisfaction of reaching that target and enjoying the fruits of their discipline.

In contrast, long-term goals are more complex and require a broader vision. They often involve significant aspirations like saving for retirement, buying a home, or funding a child's education. These goals take time to achieve and can seem daunting at first. A classic example is that of a couple saving for their children's university education, which can span over a decade. The key to success lies in consistent, incremental progress, much like planting a seed and nurturing it over the years until it bears fruit.

The science behind goal setting reveals that having both short-term and long-term goals can greatly enhance our chances of success. Research shows that breaking down a large goal into smaller, manageable tasks not only makes the journey less intimidating but also creates a sense of accomplishment along the way. This psychological boost can be vital. For instance, if someone aims to save a substantial sum for a house, setting monthly savings targets can help maintain focus and motivation, celebrating each milestone reached.

It is essential to align short-term and long-term goals to create a cohesive financial strategy. Short-term goals can serve as stepping stones towards achieving long-term aspirations. If someone's long-term goal is to retire comfortably, short-term goals could include increasing contributions to a retirement account or building an emergency fund. This alignment ensures that immediate actions are purposeful and contribute to overarching objectives, reinforcing the importance of each effort made today.

To effectively manage both types of goals, individuals should regularly review and adjust their plans. Life circumstances can change, requiring flexibility in how goals are approached. Keeping a journal or using budgeting apps can help track progress and make necessary adjustments. By sharing stories of success and setbacks, we can inspire one another to stay committed, reminding ourselves that the journey towards financial security is made up of both short bursts of effort and the long, steady march towards our ultimate dreams.

Chapter 4: Budgeting Basics

Creating a Personal Budget

Creating a personal budget is not just about numbers; it is about understanding your relationship with money. For many, budgeting feels restrictive, yet it can be liberating. When Sarah, a young professional, started tracking her expenses, she discovered she was spending far more on dining out than she realised. By reallocating those funds towards her savings, she found herself closer to her dream of travelling, which brought her immense joy. A budget can serve as a compass, guiding you toward your financial goals while allowing you to enjoy life.

The science behind budgeting is rooted in behaviour. Studies show that individuals who maintain a budget are more likely to achieve their financial goals. This is because budgeting creates awareness and accountability. When John, a middle-aged father, began budgeting with his family, they collectively understood their financial situation better. They started making informed decisions together, which not only reduced their expenses but also strengthened their family bond. The act of budgeting transformed their financial landscape into a shared journey.

To create an effective personal budget, start by identifying your income sources and categorising your expenses. Break down your spending into fixed and variable costs. Fixed costs, such as rent or mortgage, are predictable and must be accommodated in your budget. Variable costs, on the other hand, can be adjusted. By tracking these categories, you will gain insight into your spending habits. For instance, when Emma, a recent graduate, noticed her variable costs were high due to impulse purchases, she decided to set a monthly limit for discretionary spending, which significantly improved her financial stability.

Next, set realistic financial goals. Whether it's saving for a home, a holiday, or retirement, having clear goals can motivate you to stick to your budget. Visualising your goals can be particularly powerful. When Mark, a young entrepreneur, visualised owning a café, he was more disciplined with his budgeting. He created a savings plan that allocated a portion of his income towards this dream. As he saw his savings grow, so did his determination, proving that budgeting is not merely about restrictions but about empowering choices.

Finally, review and adjust your budget regularly. Life circumstances change, and so should your budget. Regular reviews allow you to stay on track and make necessary adjustments. When Lisa, a single mother, faced unexpected medical expenses, she revisited her budget to accommodate these changes. This flexibility helped her manage her finances without overwhelming stress. Embracing a budgeting mindset can transform your financial future, giving you the tools to build lasting wealth while enjoying the journey.

Tracking Your Expenses

Tracking your expenses is a crucial step towards achieving financial security. Many people live their lives without a clear understanding of where their money goes, often leading to financial stress and uncertainty. By keeping a close eye on your spending habits, you can identify areas where you can save and make more informed decisions about your finances. This practice not only promotes awareness but also helps you build a solid foundation for wealth accumulation.

Consider the story of Sarah, a young professional who felt overwhelmed by her financial situation. Each month, she found herself short on cash, despite earning a decent salary. It wasn't until she started tracking her expenses that she realised how much she was spending on non-essentials like dining out and subscription services. By simply recording her expenditures, Sarah was able to cut back on unnecessary spending and redirect those funds into savings, setting her on a path towards financial stability.

The science behind tracking expenses is simple: awareness leads to accountability. Research shows that individuals who actively monitor their spending tend to have better financial outcomes. This is because tracking creates a sense of responsibility for one's financial choices. The act of writing down expenses can serve as a reminder of your goals, making it easier to resist impulsive purchases and stick to a budget. It transforms the often abstract concept of money into something tangible and manageable.

To get started on your expense-tracking journey, all you need is a notebook or a digital app. Begin by documenting every expense, no matter how small. Categorise your spending into sections such as necessities, savings, and discretionary spending. At the end of each month, review your spending patterns. This reflection will empower you to make necessary adjustments and reinforce positive financial behaviours.

Remember, the goal is not to deprive yourself but to understand your financial habits better.

In conclusion, tracking your expenses is a powerful tool in your financial toolkit. It fosters a deeper awareness of your money habits and enables you to make informed decisions that align with your financial goals. As you embark on this journey, remember that every small step counts. Just like Sarah, you too can take control of your finances and pave the way for a secure financial future. Embrace the process, and watch as your financial landscape transforms for the better.

Chapter 5: The Importance of Saving

Building an Emergency Fund

Building an emergency fund is a crucial step in securing your financial future, yet many overlook it. Imagine the peace of mind that comes from knowing you can handle unexpected expenses without going into debt. Just ask Sarah, a single mother who, after setting aside three months' worth of expenses, faced a medical emergency with confidence rather than panic. Her story illustrates that an emergency fund is not just a financial buffer but a source of emotional strength.

The science behind saving for emergencies is compelling. Financial experts recommend saving at least three to six months' worth of living expenses. This safety net protects against life's uncertainties, such as job loss or unexpected repairs. Research shows that individuals with emergency funds report lower stress levels and greater overall satisfaction with their financial situation. This demonstrates that financial stability can lead to mental well-being, making the case for starting an emergency fund even more compelling.

To begin building your emergency fund, start by setting a realistic goal. Assess your monthly expenses and determine how much you need to save. Then, create a budget that prioritises this savings goal. For instance, if you can set aside just £50 a week, you could reach a £1,000 emergency fund in just five months. Small, consistent contributions can lead to significant savings over time, making the process manageable for anyone.

Once you've established your goal, choose a dedicated savings account that offers easy access but is separate from your everyday spending. This will help you resist the temptation to dip into your fund for non-emergencies. Many people find success by automating their savings, ensuring that a portion of their income is transferred directly into their emergency fund each month. This strategy takes the decision-making out of saving, allowing you to build your fund effortlessly.

In conclusion, building an emergency fund is not merely a financial task; it's a life-changing decision that can provide tranquillity and security. By taking small, actionable steps, anyone can create a safety net that protects against life's unpredictability. Remember, those who prepare for the unexpected often find themselves better equipped to handle whatever comes their way, making financial resilience a key component of lasting wealth.

Strategies for Effective Saving

Saving money is not just about putting aside a portion of your income; it is about cultivating a mindset that prioritises financial security and long-term goals. Take the story of Sarah, a young professional who, after a few years of struggling with her finances, realised that her lack of saving was holding her back from achieving her dreams. She began to set aside a small amount each month, no matter how insignificant it felt, and soon discovered the power of compound interest. This simple yet effective strategy transformed her financial landscape, paving the way for future investments and opportunities.

One of the most effective strategies for saving is automating your savings process. Much like setting a reminder for an important appointment, automating transfers to your savings account can ensure that you consistently save without having to think about it. James, a father of three, implemented this strategy and found that he was saving more than he ever thought possible. By treating his savings like a non-negotiable expense, he was able to build an emergency fund that provided his family with peace of mind during uncertain times.

Understanding the psychological aspects of saving can also significantly enhance your ability to save effectively. Research shows that visualising your goals—whether it's a dream holiday, a new home, or retirement—can motivate you to save more diligently. Laura, who dreamed of travelling the world, created a vision board that prominently featured her goals. This constant reminder kept her focused on saving, making sacrifices in her daily spending feel worthwhile as she was actively working towards something bigger.

Creating a budget is another essential step in effective saving. It allows you to track your income and expenses, identifying areas where you can cut back. Mark, a recent college graduate, struggled with his finances until he created a simple budget. By analysing his spending habits, he realised he was spending too much on dining out. After making a few adjustments, he redirected those funds into savings, which eventually helped him secure a down payment for his first home.

Lastly, embracing the concept of 'paying yourself first' can revolutionise your saving habits. This principle encourages you to allocate a portion of your income to savings before addressing any other expenses. Emma, a small business owner, adopted this approach and found that it fundamentally changed her financial situation. By prioritising her savings, she was not only able to weather unexpected expenses but also invest in her business, setting herself up for long-term success. These strategies, rooted in both personal stories and scientific understanding, can empower anyone seeking to achieve lasting financial stability.

Chapter 6: Understanding Debt

Types of Debt

Debt can often feel like a heavy burden, yet understanding its various forms can empower us to make informed financial decisions. There are two primary categories of debt: secured and unsecured. Secured debt is backed by collateral, which means if you fail to repay, the lender can seize the asset. A common example is a mortgage, where your home serves as security. Knowing this can help individuals appreciate the importance of managing such debt wisely to avoid losing valuable assets.

On the other hand, unsecured debt does not have collateral tied to it. Credit cards and personal loans fall into this category, representing a riskier venture for lenders. Without a safety net, interest rates on unsecured debts tend to be higher, making it critical for borrowers to maintain discipline in their spending. A story that illustrates this is of a young professional who accumulated credit card debt while trying to maintain a lifestyle beyond their means, only to face overwhelming monthly payments that stifled their financial growth.

Then we have revolving debt, such as credit cards, which allows borrowers to use and repay funds repeatedly within a credit limit. This flexibility can be beneficial but can also lead to a cycle of debt if not managed properly. A cautionary tale is that of a college student who relied on credit for everyday expenses, ultimately graduating with a significant debt load that took years to pay off. Understanding the implications of revolving debt is crucial for maintaining financial health in the long run.

Next, there's installment debt, which involves borrowing a fixed amount and repaying it in regular payments over a specified period. This type of debt is often seen in auto loans and mortgages. The predictability of these payments can make budgeting easier and provide a clear path to being debt-free. The story of a family who diligently paid off their car loan ahead of schedule illustrates how strategic management of installment debt can lead to financial freedom and peace of mind.

In conclusion, comprehending the different types of debt is essential for anyone seeking to build lasting wealth. By recognising the characteristics and implications of secured, unsecured, revolving, and installment debts, individuals can make smarter financial choices. The journey towards financial security is much like navigating a maze; understanding the types of debt can help illuminate the path forward, enabling us to avoid pitfalls and seize opportunities for wealth creation.

Strategies for Managing Debt

Managing debt can often feel like an overwhelming burden, but developing effective strategies can transform this challenge into a manageable part of your financial journey. One fundamental principle is to understand the nature of your debt. For instance, a person named Sarah found herself knee-deep in credit card debt after a series of unexpected expenses. By categorising her debts and identifying which carried the highest interest rates, she took the first step towards regaining control.

Understanding your financial obligations is crucial in crafting a personalised repayment plan.

Next, establishing a realistic budget is essential for anyone looking to manage their debt effectively. John, a recent graduate, faced student loans that seemed insurmountable. He started by tracking his monthly expenses and income, allowing him to pinpoint areas where he could cut back. This simple yet effective strategy helped him allocate more funds towards his debt each month. By adhering to a budget, individuals can not only manage their current debts but also prevent future financial pitfalls.

Another powerful strategy is to prioritise debt repayment. The snowball method, where one focuses on paying off the smallest debts first while making minimum payments on larger debts, can provide quick wins that motivate continued progress. For example, Emily paid off her smallest credit card, which gave her a sense of accomplishment and boosted her confidence. This psychological boost can be crucial in maintaining momentum toward becoming debt-free, turning the daunting task into a series of achievable goals.

Additionally, seeking professional advice can be invaluable. Many people, like Michael, have found that speaking to a financial advisor helped them navigate complex debt scenarios. Advisors can offer tailored strategies and insights based on individual circumstances, helping to create a structured plan for repayment. This step not only provides expert guidance but also reassures individuals that they are not alone in their financial struggles.

Finally, fostering a mindset of resilience and discipline is vital in the journey towards debt management. Stories of perseverance abound, such as that of Lisa, who, after years of working multiple jobs, finally became debt-free. Her journey highlights that commitment and determination can lead to financial freedom. By embracing a long-term perspective and celebrating small victories along the way, anyone can develop the discipline needed to manage and ultimately eliminate their debt, paving the way for a secure financial future.

Chapter 7: Investing for the Future

Introduction to Investing

Investing is not merely a financial activity; it is a journey towards securing a prosperous future. Many people view it as a daunting task reserved for the wealthy or the highly educated, yet investing is accessible to everyone. Consider the story of a single mother who, with a modest income, began investing in her first mutual fund. Over time, her small contributions grew, illustrating that starting small can lead to significant results. This journey of investing is about making informed decisions that can ultimately change lives.

At its core, investing is about making your money work for you. The fundamental principles of investing apply universally, regardless of your background or financial status. Scientific studies have shown that even the simplest investment strategies can yield impressive returns over time. For instance, dollar-cost averaging, which involves regularly investing a fixed amount, can mitigate the effects of market volatility and enhance long-term growth. This reinforces the idea that consistent, disciplined investing is often more effective than trying to time the market.

Emotional resilience plays a crucial role in successful investing. Many investors are swayed by fear and greed, leading to impulsive decisions that can derail their financial goals. By cultivating a mindset focused on long-term objectives, individuals can navigate the ups and downs of the market with greater confidence. The story of an investor who held onto his stocks through market crashes, only to see them recover and flourish, exemplifies the importance of patience and perseverance in the investing landscape.

Another key aspect of investing is understanding the power of compounding. Albert Einstein famously referred to it as the eighth wonder of the world, and for good reason. The earlier one starts investing, the more time their money has to grow. A young professional who begins investing early, even with modest amounts, can amass significant wealth over decades. This highlights the importance of starting as soon as possible, regardless of the sum involved, as time is a critical ally in the wealth-building process.

Lastly, education and continuous learning are vital in the investing realm. The more informed an investor is, the better decisions they can make. Engaging with financial literature, attending workshops, or even seeking advice from seasoned investors can empower individuals to enhance their financial literacy. A community of investors sharing knowledge and experiences can create a supportive atmosphere that fosters growth and understanding. By embracing the principles of investing, anyone can embark on the path to timeless wealth, transforming not just their financial future but their entire lives.

Different Types of Investments

Investing is a vital part of building wealth, and understanding the different types of investments can empower individuals to make informed decisions. From stocks and bonds to real estate and mutual funds, each investment type comes with its own set of risks and rewards. For instance, consider the story of Sarah, a young professional who began her investment journey by purchasing shares in a technology company. Through research and patience, her initial investment grew significantly, illustrating the potential of the stock market to generate wealth over time.

Bonds represent another investment avenue, often seen as a safer option compared to stocks. When John, a retired teacher, invested in government bonds, he found peace of mind knowing that he would receive regular interest payments. This steady income allowed him to enjoy his retirement without financial stress. Understanding bonds can be particularly crucial for those seeking stability in their investment portfolio, especially in uncertain economic times.

Real estate is another powerful investment type, often considered a cornerstone for building lasting wealth. Take the example of Emma, who purchased a modest property in her neighbourhood. Over the years, the value of her home appreciated, and by renting out a portion, she created an additional income stream. Real estate not only provides the potential for capital appreciation but also offers tax advantages and the satisfaction of owning tangible assets.

Mutual funds and exchange-traded funds (ETFs) present a chance for investors to diversify their portfolios with ease. With these investment vehicles, individuals can pool their money with others to invest in a variety of assets, thus spreading risk. When Mark decided to invest in a mutual fund, he appreciated the professional management and diversification it offered. This allowed him to focus on his career while still fostering his financial growth.

Lastly, alternative investments such as cryptocurrencies and peer-to-peer lending have gained popularity in recent years. While they come with higher risks, they also offer unique opportunities for significant returns. For instance, Lisa invested in cryptocurrency during its early stages and saw her investment multiply. However, it's essential for investors to conduct thorough research and understand the market dynamics before venturing into these less traditional options.

Chapter 8: The Role of Insurance

Protecting Your Assets

In today's unpredictable world, protecting your assets is more crucial than ever. Imagine a young couple, Sarah and Tom, who worked tirelessly to save for their dream home. After years of sacrifice, they finally bought their house, only to face unexpected financial challenges. This story is not unique; many individuals find themselves unprepared for the storms of life. The first rule of asset protection is to be proactive rather than reactive. Planning ahead can make all the difference in safeguarding your wealth.

One effective strategy for asset protection is diversification. Just as an investor would not place all their savings into a single stock, individuals should not rely solely on one type of asset. Consider Anna, a small business owner who invested in various ventures, from real estate to stocks. When one sector faced a downturn, her diversified portfolio ensured her financial stability. This principle of spreading risk is a timeless rule that anyone can apply to their financial strategy.

Another vital step is creating an emergency fund. This fund acts as a financial buffer, allowing you to weather unforeseen circumstances without jeopardising your long-term investments. For instance, when David lost his job unexpectedly, he was grateful for the emergency savings he had built over time. This fund provided him with the peace of mind to search for new employment without the pressure of immediate financial distress. Building an emergency fund is a cornerstone of financial security that everyone should consider.

Insurance is also an essential tool for protecting your assets. Many people overlook the importance of adequate insurance coverage. Take, for example, the case of Lisa, who had her home insured just as a precaution. When a fire devastated her property, her insurance policy allowed her to rebuild and recover without incurring crippling debt. Understanding the different types of insurance and ensuring you are properly covered can protect your wealth from unforeseen disasters.

Lastly, consider the value of legal protection through estate planning. This often-overlooked aspect can safeguard your assets for future generations. Think of the Johnson family, who created a trust to manage their wealth. This not only protected their assets from unnecessary taxes but also ensured their children would inherit their wealth seamlessly. Estate planning is not just for the wealthy; it is a crucial step for anyone wishing to secure their financial legacy for the future.

Understanding Different Types of Insurance

Understanding different types of insurance is vital for securing your financial future. Insurance serves as a safety net, protecting you against unforeseen circumstances that could otherwise lead to financial ruin. Take the story of Jane, a single mother who faced a sudden illness. Thanks to her health insurance, she was able to focus on recovery without the added stress of overwhelming medical bills. This highlights how selecting the right insurance can be a life-changing decision.

There are various types of insurance, each serving a unique purpose. Health insurance covers medical expenses, while life insurance provides financial security for your loved ones in case of your untimely demise. Homeowners insurance protects your property against damages, and auto insurance covers liabilities arising from car accidents. By understanding these categories, you can tailor your insurance portfolio to fit your specific needs, ensuring comprehensive protection.

The science behind insurance is rooted in risk management. Insurance companies assess risks and calculate premiums based on the likelihood of certain events occurring. For instance, younger drivers often pay higher premiums due to their inexperience, while older drivers may receive discounts for their track record. This statistical approach allows individuals to make informed decisions about which types of insurance they need, balancing coverage with affordability.

When considering insurance options, it is crucial to evaluate your personal circumstances and priorities. Create a list of potential risks you face and the financial implications of those risks. For example, if you own a home, consider the costs of repairs or replacement in the event of damage. By identifying these factors, you can better understand which insurance policies will provide the necessary protection for your assets and loved ones.

Ultimately, understanding different types of insurance empowers you to make informed choices that contribute to your overall financial health. Just as Jane learned to appreciate the importance of her health insurance, you too can take proactive steps to safeguard your wealth. By investing time in understanding insurance, you can build a solid foundation for your financial future, ensuring peace of mind and security for yourself and your family.

Chapter 9: The Impact of Taxes

Understanding Tax Obligations

Understanding tax obligations is a cornerstone of financial literacy and a vital aspect of building lasting wealth. Imagine a young entrepreneur named Sarah, who, after launching her own business, is excited about her success but finds herself overwhelmed by tax forms and deadlines. Like many, she initially viewed taxes as a burden, but as she began to learn about her obligations, she realised that they are not just a requirement but a crucial aspect of her financial strategy. Understanding taxes can empower individuals to make informed decisions that enhance their financial stability and growth.

At the core of understanding tax obligations is the recognition that taxes fund essential services and infrastructure. Consider the story of a community that came together to improve local schools and roads, funded by the taxes paid by its residents. This perspective can shift the narrative from viewing taxes as a drain on income to seeing them as an investment in society. By understanding where tax money goes, individuals can feel more engaged and responsible in their financial dealings, reinforcing the idea that paying taxes is part of contributing to a greater good.

Furthermore, the science of tax regulations can be complex, but breaking it down into manageable steps can demystify the process. One effective approach is to keep detailed records throughout the year, allowing taxpayers to accurately report income and claim deductions. For instance, an artist might keep receipts for art supplies and exhibition fees, which can substantially lower her taxable income. By establishing a system for tracking expenses, individuals can navigate their tax obligations with confidence, turning what once felt daunting into a straightforward task.

Additionally, seeking professional advice can be a game changer in understanding tax obligations. Many people, like John, a small business owner who struggled with his taxes, discovered the value of hiring an accountant. With the right guidance, John learned about tax credits and benefits that he had previously overlooked. This not only eased his financial burden but also opened new avenues for investment in his business. Engaging with a tax professional can provide clarity and ensure that individuals are making the most of their financial resources while staying compliant with regulations.

Ultimately, embracing a proactive approach to tax obligations is essential for anyone aiming to build lasting wealth. By educating themselves, maintaining proper records, and seeking professional guidance, individuals can transform their relationship with taxes from one of anxiety to one of empowerment. As Sarah, John, and many others demonstrate, understanding tax obligations is not merely about compliance; it's about utilising them as tools for achieving financial success and security in an ever-changing world.

Strategies for Tax Efficiency

Achieving tax efficiency is a vital component of building lasting wealth, yet many overlook its significance. Consider the story of Sarah, a small business owner who discovered that strategic tax planning allowed her to reinvest more into her business. By utilising available deductions and credits, she not only maximised her earnings but also paved a smoother path for growth. This illustrates how understanding tax laws can transform your financial landscape, allowing you to keep more of what you earn and use it to build your future.

One effective strategy for tax efficiency is to invest in tax-advantaged accounts. For instance, retirement accounts like IRAs and 401(k)s in the US, or ISAs in the UK, offer significant tax benefits. The science behind this is compelling; these accounts allow your investments to grow tax-free or tax-deferred, meaning you can accumulate wealth more effectively over time. By contributing to these accounts, you are not only saving for the future but also strategically reducing your taxable income today.

Another crucial strategy is to be mindful of your capital gains. When you sell an investment for more than you paid, the profit is subject to capital gains tax. However, consider the case of Tom, who held onto his investments for over a year, allowing them to qualify for long-term capital gains rates. By adopting a buy-and-hold strategy, Tom effectively reduced his tax burden while still enjoying the benefits of his investments. This approach demonstrates that patience can be as rewarding financially as it is emotionally.

Additionally, charitable contributions can provide dual benefits; they support worthy causes while also reducing your taxable income. For example, Emily decided to donate a portion of her earnings to a local charity. Not only did she feel fulfilled by giving back, but she also enjoyed a tax deduction that lightened her financial load. This illustrates the emotional and financial rewards of aligning your values with your financial strategies, creating a win-win situation.

Finally, consulting with a tax professional can yield substantial benefits. A good advisor can help you identify intricate tax-saving opportunities that you might miss on your own. Like the story of Mark, who discovered hidden deductions that reduced his tax liability significantly, working with an expert can empower you to make informed choices. In the end, employing these strategies not only enhances your financial well-being but also brings peace of mind, knowing you are making the most of your wealth.

Chapter 10: Building Wealth Through Multiple Streams

Identifying Opportunities

In the journey towards financial security, identifying opportunities is akin to discovering hidden treasures. Many individuals overlook the potential that lies within their own circumstances, often waiting for a significant change or stroke of luck. However, the truth is that opportunities are all around us, waiting to be recognised and seized. For instance, consider the story of a young entrepreneur who turned a simple hobby of baking into a thriving business, illustrating how personal passions can transform into profitable ventures.

Understanding the science behind opportunity recognition can be empowering. Research indicates that those who actively seek out opportunities are more likely to succeed. This can be achieved through a mindset shift that encourages curiosity and openness to new experiences. A practical step is to keep a journal, noting down ideas and inspirations as they arise, providing a valuable resource for future reference. This method not only fosters creativity but also builds a habit of recognising potential in everyday situations.

Moreover, networking plays a crucial role in identifying opportunities. Engaging with diverse groups of people can broaden one's perspective and expose individuals to ideas they may not have encountered otherwise. For example, attending community workshops or industry conferences can lead to unexpected collaborations or insights that may spark new ventures. By actively participating in these environments, individuals can cultivate a rich network that serves as a fertile ground for opportunity.

Another method to uncover opportunities is through continuous learning. The world is constantly evolving, and staying informed about trends and innovations can provide a competitive edge. Whether it's reading articles, taking online courses, or listening to podcasts, committing to lifelong learning equips individuals with the knowledge to spot and act on potential opportunities. The story of a tech professional who reskilled during a market shift exemplifies how adaptability can lead to new career paths and financial growth.

Finally, it is essential to cultivate resilience and a positive mindset in the face of challenges. Recognising that setbacks are a natural part of the journey can help individuals maintain their focus on long-term goals. Embracing a growth mindset encourages people to view failures as learning experiences, ultimately paving the way for future successes. By following these steps, anyone can enhance their ability to identify and seize opportunities, thus embarking on their timeless path to wealth.

Passive vs Active Income

The distinction between passive and active income is crucial for anyone striving for financial security. Active income is earned through direct efforts, like a job where you exchange time for money. This method can be satisfying but often leads to a cycle of working harder without a proportional increase in wealth. For instance, consider Sarah, a dedicated teacher who loves her job yet finds herself unable to save significantly despite long hours and holidays spent tutoring. Sarah's situation highlights the limitations of relying solely on active income.

On the other hand, passive income offers a pathway to financial freedom by allowing money to work for you. This income is generated from investments, royalties, or rental properties that require little to no effort once set up. Take the story of John, who invested in rental properties. Over time, John found that his properties generated consistent income, allowing him to spend more time with his family and pursue hobbies. His journey illustrates the power of passive income in providing not just financial security but also a richer life experience.

The science behind these income types is compelling. Research shows that individuals with diverse income streams tend to experience lower stress levels and greater life satisfaction. A study conducted by financial institutions revealed that those with passive income sources reported feeling more secure about their financial futures. This evidence supports the idea that building passive income is not just a strategy for wealth accumulation but a foundation for a more balanced and fulfilling life.

To transition from active to passive income, one must take deliberate steps. Start by assessing your skills and interests to identify potential passive income opportunities. You might consider investing in stocks, creating digital products, or starting a side business that can operate without your constant involvement. The key lies in setting up systems that generate income with minimal daily effort. As you embark on this journey, remember that patience and persistence are essential; building a robust passive income stream takes time and effort initially.

Ultimately, the journey from active to passive income is about empowerment. It allows individuals to reclaim their time and invest it in what truly matters to them. Embracing both income types can lead to a balanced financial life, where one does not solely rely on work for survival. As you reflect on your financial goals, consider how you can integrate passive income strategies into your life, paving the way for a more secure and enriching future.

Chapter 11: The Importance of Financial Planning

Creating a Financial Plan

Creating a financial plan is akin to crafting a roadmap for your life. It provides direction, clarity, and purpose, allowing you to navigate the complexities of earning, saving, and investing. Consider the story of Sarah, a young professional who found herself overwhelmed with student debt and living paycheck to paycheck. By developing a financial plan, she set achievable goals, tracked her expenses, and reallocated her spending towards savings and investments, ultimately transforming her financial situation.

The science behind financial planning is grounded in behavioural economics, which suggests that individuals are often motivated by both rational and emotional factors. Understanding this can empower you to create a plan that aligns with your values and aspirations. Take a page from the experiences of John, a family man who realised that his spending habits were deeply tied to his emotions. By acknowledging this connection, he was able to create a budget that not only catered to his family's needs but also included provisions for family activities that enhanced their emotional well-being.

To embark on the journey of financial planning, one must first assess their current financial health. This involves taking stock of income, expenses, debts, and assets. For example, Emma, a freelance artist, began her planning by meticulously documenting her monthly income and the fluctuating nature of her expenses. This step allowed her to identify areas of unnecessary spending and focus on building a financial cushion for future uncertainties.

Next, setting clear and realistic financial goals is crucial. Whether it's saving for a home, planning for retirement, or setting up an emergency fund, these goals should be specific, measurable, achievable, relevant, and time-bound (SMART). Mark, an engineer, set a five-year goal to save for a deposit on his first house. By breaking this larger goal into smaller, manageable milestones, he was able to stay motivated and track his progress effectively.

Finally, regularly reviewing and adjusting your financial plan is essential to ensure it remains relevant as life circumstances change. Life events such as marriage, parenthood, or career changes can significantly impact your financial situation. For instance, when Lisa became a mother, she revisited her financial plan to accommodate her new responsibilities. By remaining adaptable and proactive, Lisa ensured that her financial plan continually served her needs, paving the way for a secure financial future.

Reviewing and Adjusting Your Plan

In the journey towards financial security, reviewing and adjusting your plan is not merely an option; it is a necessity. Life is unpredictable, and unforeseen circumstances can arise at any moment. For instance, consider the story of a young couple who meticulously saved for their dream home. Just when they were ready to purchase, a sudden job loss forced them to reevaluate their financial strategy. By regularly reviewing their plan, they were able to adapt and ultimately achieve their goal, albeit with new timelines and priorities.

The science of behavioural finance suggests that emotions significantly influence our financial decisions. When we allow our feelings to dictate our actions, we may drift away from our established financial paths. An example of this is someone who, after experiencing a windfall, decides to splurge rather than reassess their long-term goals. By incorporating regular check-ins into your financial planning, you can remain grounded and focused, ensuring your decisions are aligned with your ultimate objectives.

To effectively review your financial plan, start by setting specific intervals for evaluation—be it quarterly or bi-annually. During these sessions, assess your progress against your original goals. Are you on track to meet your savings targets? Have your expenses changed, and if so, how does that affect your financial plan? This structured approach not only provides clarity but also instils a sense of accountability that can motivate you to stay on course.

Adjustments to your plan should not be viewed as failures but as essential pivots in your financial strategy. Just like a seasoned sailor who must adjust their sails to navigate changing winds, you too must be willing to adapt. For example, if your investment choices are underperforming, consider reallocating your assets to more promising opportunities. Embracing these changes can lead to greater financial rewards and a more resilient plan in the long run.

Ultimately, the act of reviewing and adjusting your financial plan is about fostering a mindset of growth and adaptability. Each assessment is an opportunity to learn from past experiences and make informed decisions for the future. As you navigate your unique financial journey, remember that flexibility is key. By embracing change and committing to your financial well-being, you are setting the foundation for a secure and prosperous future.

Chapter 12: Leaving a Legacy

The Importance of Estate Planning

Estate planning is a crucial aspect of financial security that often gets overlooked. Many individuals assume that only the wealthy need to worry about it, but this is a misconception. In reality, estate planning affects everyone, regardless of their financial status. It's about ensuring that your desires are fulfilled after your passing and that your loved ones are taken care of. Without a solid plan in place, the state can impose its own rules on your assets, potentially leading to unnecessary complications and emotional stress for your family.

Consider the story of a middle-class family who lost their father unexpectedly. He had not created a will, and as a result, his assets were frozen in a lengthy legal battle. The family was left in a precarious situation, forced to navigate the complexities of the probate process while grieving their loss. This scenario highlights the importance of making decisions about your estate while you can still express your wishes clearly. By taking the time to plan, you can spare your loved ones from added burdens during an already difficult time.

Scientific studies show that individuals who engage in estate planning often report feeling a greater sense of control and peace of mind. This sense of empowerment comes from knowing that their wishes will be respected and their loved ones will be provided for. Moreover, proper estate planning can lead to significant tax savings and a smoother transition of wealth. The psychological benefits of feeling organised and prepared cannot be overstated, as they contribute to overall well-being and financial stability.

To embark on the path of effective estate planning, start by assessing your current financial situation. List your assets, liabilities, and any specific wishes you have for their distribution. Next, consider consulting with an estate planning attorney who can guide you through the legal requirements and help you create a will or trust that reflects your desires. Regularly reviewing and updating your estate plan is essential, especially after major life events such as marriage, divorce, or the birth of a child.

In conclusion, estate planning is not merely a task for the affluent; it is a vital process for everyone. By taking the necessary steps to plan your estate, you can safeguard your family's future, alleviate potential conflicts, and ensure that your legacy is honoured. Remember, the time to plan is now—don't leave your loved ones navigating uncertainty in your absence. Start today, and secure the peace of mind that comes with knowing you've taken control of your financial legacy.

Teaching Future Generations

Teaching future generations about wealth is not merely a financial lesson; it is a gift that can transform lives. Imagine a young child learning to save their pocket money, gradually understanding the value of every penny. This simple act of saving can lay the foundation for a lifetime of financial wisdom. By instilling these principles early, we empower our children to make informed decisions in an often overwhelming financial landscape.

Storytelling plays a crucial role in this educational journey. Consider the story of a grandmother who, during the Great Depression, taught her grandchildren how to budget with limited resources. Through her tales of resilience and resourcefulness, she not only provided practical skills but also imparted critical life lessons about the importance of living within one's means. Such narratives resonate deeply, illustrating that financial literacy is not just about numbers but also about the values we hold.

Science supports the idea that financial behaviours are often learned rather than innate. Research shows that children who are taught about money management tend to develop healthier financial habits as adults. Moreover, by involving them in discussions about finances—such as family budgeting or planning for a holiday—parents can demystify money. These conversations can foster an environment where financial literacy is a natural part of growing up, rather than a daunting subject introduced only in adulthood.

To teach future generations effectively, we must adopt a structured approach. Start with simple concepts like saving and spending, then gradually introduce more complex ideas such as investing and financial planning. Encourage children to set their own financial goals and celebrate their achievements, no matter how small. This step-by-step method not only makes learning engaging but also instils a sense of ownership over their financial futures.

Ultimately, teaching future generations about wealth is an investment in society as a whole. When we equip young people with the knowledge and skills to manage their finances, we are cultivating a more informed and responsible citizenry. As they grow into adulthood, these individuals will be better prepared to face financial challenges, contribute to their communities, and pave the way for others. The cycle of teaching and learning about wealth can create a legacy of financial security that endures for generations to come.

Chapter 13: Overcoming Financial Obstacles

Common Challenges

In the journey towards financial security, many individuals encounter common challenges that can hinder their progress. One prevalent obstacle is the fear of taking risks. This fear often stems from stories of others who have lost everything in investments or failed businesses. However, embracing calculated risks is essential for wealth creation. Understanding the balance between risk and reward, and learning from the experiences of others, can empower individuals to make informed decisions that propel them forward.

Another significant challenge is the overwhelming amount of information available today. With countless financial advice articles, books, and seminars, it can be difficult to discern which strategies are effective and applicable to one's unique situation. To navigate this sea of information, individuals should focus on the fundamentals of financial literacy. Engaging with trusted sources, seeking mentorship, and simplifying goals into actionable steps can help demystify the path to wealth.

Additionally, many people struggle with the discipline required to manage their finances consistently. The allure of immediate gratification often overshadows long-term planning. Stories of individuals who achieved financial freedom by prioritising saving and investing serve as powerful reminders of the benefits of delayed gratification. Establishing a budget, setting savings goals, and creating a timeline for financial milestones can foster the discipline needed for sustained wealth-building.

Furthermore, emotional factors such as self-doubt and societal pressure can derail one's financial aspirations. The narratives we tell ourselves about money can shape our behaviours and choices. For instance, a person might believe they are not capable of financial success due to past failures or comparisons with wealthier peers. Recognising and challenging these negative beliefs is crucial. Building a supportive network and celebrating small victories can help to cultivate a positive mindset towards wealth.

Lastly, unexpected life events can disrupt even the best-laid financial plans. From medical emergencies to job losses, these occurrences can create significant financial strain. Developing an emergency fund and maintaining flexibility in financial planning can provide a buffer against life's uncertainties. Understanding that challenges are a natural part of the journey allows individuals to approach their financial goals with resilience and adaptability, ultimately leading to a more secure financial future.

Strategies for Resilience

Resilience is not merely about bouncing back from setbacks; it is about growth through adversity. Many successful individuals have faced significant challenges, yet their stories often reflect a common thread: they used their struggles as a stepping stone to greater achievements. Take the tale of J.K. Rowling, for instance. Before she became a household name,

Rowling faced rejection after rejection, battling depression and financial hardship. Her resilience allowed her to turn her life around, ultimately creating a global phenomenon. This illustrates that resilience is a vital strategy for anyone seeking to build lasting wealth.

One effective strategy for cultivating resilience is developing a growth mindset. This concept, popularised by psychologist Carol Dweck, suggests that embracing challenges and viewing failures as opportunities for learning can significantly enhance our ability to cope with adversity. Research shows that individuals with a growth mindset are more likely to persist in the face of difficulties, leading to greater success in their pursuits. By adopting this mindset, we can redefine our relationship with failure and view it as an essential part of the journey toward financial security.

Another important aspect of resilience is having a supportive community. Surrounding ourselves with positive influences can provide the encouragement we need during tough times. For example, consider the story of a small business owner who faced bankruptcy. Instead of giving up, she sought help from a local business group. Through shared experiences and advice, she was able to pivot her business model, ultimately thriving. This highlights how connection and support from others can fortify our resilience and enhance our capacity to overcome financial setbacks.

Practical steps can also bolster our resilience. Setting realistic goals and breaking them down into manageable tasks allows us to maintain focus and motivation. Additionally, cultivating healthy habits, such as regular exercise and mindfulness practices, can improve our emotional well-being and increase our ability to handle stress. Research consistently supports the link between physical health and mental resilience, suggesting that taking care of our bodies can empower us to navigate financial uncertainties more effectively.

Finally, it is essential to remember that resilience is a journey, not a destination. Each setback offers a lesson that can ultimately lead us toward our goals. By reflecting on our experiences and acknowledging our growth, we can reinforce our resilience. Embracing this ongoing process allows us to build a solid foundation for financial success. In the end, we all have the potential to cultivate resilience, transforming challenges into opportunities on our path to lasting wealth.

Chapter 14: The Emotional Side of Money

Understanding Money Mindset

Understanding Money Mindset is crucial for anyone aiming to build lasting wealth. It begins with recognising that our beliefs about money shape our financial behaviours. Many individuals grow up in environments where money is a source of stress or conflict. For instance, someone raised in a household that viewed wealth as inherently negative may subconsciously avoid financial success, leading to a cycle of poverty. Conversely, those who see money as a tool for freedom and opportunity tend to make more proactive financial choices.

Research in psychology reveals that our mindset can significantly affect our financial outcomes. The concept of a 'growth mindset', popularised by psychologist Carol Dweck, emphasises the idea that we can develop our abilities through dedication and hard work. When applied to finances, this means viewing financial challenges as opportunities for learning rather than insurmountable obstacles. By adopting a growth mindset, individuals can cultivate resilience in their financial journeys, enabling them to overcome setbacks and seize opportunities.

To shift towards a positive money mindset, it is essential to take actionable steps. Start by writing down your beliefs about money, both positive and negative. Reflect on how these beliefs influence your spending, saving, and investing habits.

This self-awareness is the first step towards change. Additionally, surrounding yourself with positive financial role models can inspire you to adopt healthier attitudes towards wealth. Engaging in communities that encourage financial literacy can also reinforce these new beliefs.

Stories of individuals who transformed their financial situations are powerful motivators. Take the example of a young entrepreneur who started with nothing but a passion for baking. Through careful budgeting, seeking mentorship, and embracing a mindset focused on growth, she turned her small home-based business into a thriving bakery. Her journey illustrates that with the right mindset and practical steps, anyone can achieve financial success, regardless of their starting point.

Ultimately, understanding your money mindset is about recognising the power of your thoughts and beliefs. By consciously choosing to cultivate a positive relationship with money, you can build a foundation for lasting wealth. Remember, it's not just about accumulating riches; it's about creating a life filled with opportunities, freedom, and security. Each step taken towards a healthier money mindset is a step towards a more secure financial future for yourself and your loved ones.

The Impact of Emotions on Financial Decisions

Emotions play a significant role in financial decision-making, often leading individuals to make choices that may not align with their long-term goals. Consider the story of a young investor who, driven by the excitement of a market rally, poured all his savings into a trending stock. Initially, the investment flourished, reinforcing his belief in emotional decision-making. However, when the market corrected, he faced devastating losses that could have been avoided had he approached his investments with a calmer, more analytical mindset.

Research in behavioural finance shows that emotional responses can cloud judgement, leading to impulsive decisions. For instance, fear can cause investors to panic and sell during downturns, while overconfidence may lead to excessive risk-taking during bullish markets. These emotional reactions often result in a cycle of buying high and selling low, which is detrimental to wealth accumulation. Understanding these emotional triggers is essential for anyone seeking to build lasting financial stability.

To navigate the emotional landscape of finance, one can employ several practical steps. Firstly, setting clear financial goals can help create a roadmap that guides decisions, reducing the influence of momentary feelings. Secondly, maintaining a diversified portfolio can mitigate the fear of loss; knowing that not all investments are tied to a single market movement can help maintain composure during volatility. Lastly, practising mindfulness and emotional awareness can foster a more rational approach to investing.

Moreover, incorporating stories of everyday people can make the lessons more relatable. Take, for example, a middle-aged couple who had to choose between following their friends into risky investments or sticking to their conservative strategy. By remembering their long-term objectives and the importance of patience, they chose the latter, ultimately reaping the benefits of steady growth rather than succumbing to the fleeting thrills of emotional trading.

In conclusion, the impact of emotions on financial decisions is profound, but by recognising these influences and applying practical strategies, individuals can cultivate a more secure financial future. Embracing a disciplined approach while remaining aware of emotional triggers can empower anyone on their journey to wealth. Remember, the path to financial success is not just about numbers; it is also about understanding oneself and making decisions that align with one's true aspirations.

Chapter 15: The Timeless Wealth Principles

Recap of Key Lessons

In the journey towards financial security, understanding the key lessons is paramount. One of the most significant lessons is the power of compounding. Consider the story of a young woman named Sarah, who started investing small amounts in her twenties. By the time she reached retirement, her investments had multiplied significantly, illustrating how starting early can lead to substantial wealth over time. This principle, supported by numerous studies, emphasises that time in the market is more beneficial than timing the market.

Another vital lesson is the importance of budgeting. Take the example of a family who struggled financially until they began tracking their expenses. By creating a budget, they identified unnecessary expenditures and redirected those funds towards savings and investments. This simple step not only improved their financial situation but also provided them with peace of mind. Science shows that individuals who maintain a budget are more likely to achieve their financial goals, reinforcing the necessity of this practice.

Diversification is another key lesson that cannot be overlooked. A tale often shared is that of an investor who placed all their savings into a single stock, only to face devastating losses when the company faltered. In contrast, those who spread their investments across various assets enjoyed more stability and growth. Research indicates that a well-diversified portfolio can mitigate risks and enhance returns, making it a critical strategy for anyone seeking lasting wealth.

Moreover, the emotional aspect of wealth-building is crucial. Many individuals are driven by fear or greed, leading to impulsive financial decisions. The story of a man who sold all his investments during a market dip only to watch them recover illustrates the need for emotional resilience. Scientific studies suggest that emotional intelligence can significantly impact financial decision-making, highlighting the importance of cultivating a balanced mindset when it comes to wealth.

Lastly, continuous learning and adapting are essential on the path to financial security. The world of finance is ever-changing, and staying informed can make all the difference. Consider the example of a retiree who actively sought new knowledge about investment strategies, allowing them to grow their savings even after retirement. This commitment to lifelong learning is supported by research, which shows that those who adapt to new information are more likely to thrive financially. Embracing these key lessons will set anyone on a timeless path to wealth.

Living by the Rules of Timeless Wealth

In today's fast-paced world, adhering to the principles of timeless wealth can set individuals apart from the crowd. These principles are not merely theoretical; they are grounded in the experiences of those who have successfully navigated the financial landscape. Consider the story of a humble schoolteacher who, despite earning a modest salary, diligently saved and invested wisely. Over decades, her small, consistent contributions compounded, transforming her financial situation into one of stability and security. This narrative exemplifies how living by the rules can cultivate a wealth that is both enduring and resilient.

Science supports the notion that consistency and disciplined financial habits are paramount to success. Research indicates that individuals who maintain a regular savings schedule and invest in diversified portfolios are more likely to achieve financial independence. The power of compounding interest means that even small amounts, if saved consistently over time, can lead to substantial wealth accumulation. By understanding these scientific principles, anyone can take actionable steps towards their financial goals, reinforcing the idea that wealth is not reserved for the elite but is attainable for all.

The steps to living by the rules of timeless wealth are straightforward and accessible. Firstly, create a budget that reflects your priorities and ensures that savings are a non-negotiable part of your financial plan. Secondly, educate yourself about investment options and consider seeking advice from financial professionals. The knowledge gained will empower you to make informed choices. Lastly, practice patience; wealth building is a marathon, not a sprint. Embracing this mindset can alleviate pressure and foster a more enjoyable financial journey.

Moreover, it is essential to cultivate a wealth mindset that embraces growth and learning. Regularly reflecting on your financial decisions and seeking continuous improvement can lead to better outcomes. The story of a young entrepreneur who faced multiple failures before eventually launching a successful startup illustrates this principle beautifully. Each setback was a lesson learned, contributing to his eventual triumph and demonstrating that resilience is key to financial success.

Ultimately, living by the rules of timeless wealth involves a commitment to lifelong learning and adaptability. As the financial landscape evolves, so too must our strategies and mindsets. By embracing these timeless principles, anyone can craft a secure financial future that withstands the tests of time. The journey may present challenges, but with determination and the right rules, it is a journey worth undertaking for a lifetime of financial security. It's a beautiful day

AUTHOR RICHARD TRILLION Mantey

www.ingramcontent.com/pod-product-compliance
Lightning Source LLC
LaVergne TN
LVHW022321200926
848481LV00004B/1383

* 9 7 9 8 8 9 9 7 9 7 1 7 0 *